Fossilized!
INSECT FOSSILS

By Kathleen Connors

Gareth Stevens
Publishing

Please visit our website, www.garethstevens.com. For a free color catalog of all our high-quality books, call toll free 1-800-542-2595 or fax 1-877-542-2596.

Library of Congress Cataloging-in-Publication Data

Connors, Kathleen.
Insect fossils / Kathleen Connors.
    p. cm. — (Fossilized!)
Includes index.
ISBN 978-1-4339-6418-3 (pbk.)
ISBN 978-1-4339-6419-0 (6-pack)
ISBN 978-1-4339-6416-9 (library binding)
1. Insects, Fossil—Juvenile literature. I. Title.
QE831.C66 2012
565'.7—dc23

                                        2011020899

First Edition

Published in 2013 by
Gareth Stevens Publishing
111 East 14th Street, Suite 349
New York, NY 10003

Copyright © 2013 Gareth Stevens Publishing

Designer: Katelyn E. Reynolds
Editor: Kristen Rajczak

Photo credits: Cover, pp. 1, 13 John Cancalosi/National Geographic/Getty Images; pp. 4, 14–15, (cover, pp. 1, 3–24 background and graphics) Shutterstock.com; p. 5 O. Louis Mazzatenta/National Geographic/Getty Images; pp. 7, 16 iStockphoto.com; pp. 8, 21 Colin Keates/Dorling Kindersley/Getty Images; p. 9 Andreas Feininger/Time Life Pictures/ Getty Images; p. 11 De Agostini Picture Library/De Agostini/Getty Images; pp. 12, 17 iStockphoto/Thinkstock; p. 19 Steven L. Raymer/National Geographic/Getty Images; p. 20 Hemera/Thinkstock.

Printed in the United States of America

CPSIA compliance information: Batch #CW12GS: For further information contact Gareth Stevens, New York, New York at 1-800-542-2595.

CONTENTS

Words in the glossary appear in **bold** type the first time they are used in the text.

INCREDIBLE INSECTS

What do an ant and a butterfly have in common? Both are insects! Insects are small animals with a three-part body and six legs. Most have wings. About 1 million known insect **species** exist. They're found all over the world.

Fossils teach scientists about the **evolution** of insects. Fossils are the **preserved** remains or marks of plants and animals that lived thousands or millions of years ago. The oldest insect fossils are about 400 million years old!

Fossils show that ants have been around for about 100 million years. ▶

This fossil of a beetle was found in China.

FOUND FOSSILS

Many insects you know have been around since before the dinosaurs! Paleontologists have found fossils of early flies, dragonflies, grasshoppers, and many other insects. These fossils show that some insects used to be much bigger than they are now. Ancient dragonflies had a wingspan of almost 20 inches (51 cm)!

Fossilized butterflies and moths have also been found all over the world. Butterfly fossils aren't common, but the marks left by ancient butterflies look much like the beautiful insects we know today.

THE FOSSIL RECORD

Paleontologists are scientists who study the past using fossils.

This dragonfly fossil looks a lot like a modern dragonfly. ▼

ARTHROPODS

Insects are part of a group of animals called arthropods. Arthropods have an **exoskeleton** made of hard matter called chitin. Chitin is sometimes all that remains of an ancient insect or other arthropod. Soft body parts inside the animal break down, leaving only the hard exoskeleton behind as a fossil.

Some of the most common arthropod fossils come from ocean animals called trilobites. The earliest trilobites lived about 540 million years ago. Trilobites shed their exoskeletons as they grew. Many of these exoskeletons became fossilized.

Although crabs are arthropods, their fossils are uncommon. Their shells fall apart easily after death.

THE FOSSIL RECORD

Spiders, crabs, shrimp, and centipedes are arthropods.

This trilobite fossil is about 500 million years old!

INSECT TIMELINE

Fossils help scientists figure out how insects became what they are today. You might think there would be plenty of fossils since millions of insects have lived on Earth. However, their exoskeletons often weren't preserved because the conditions weren't right for fossilization.

As a result, there are many gaps in the timeline of insect evolution. We have not yet found insect fossils from about 385 million to 318 million years ago. Scientists have to **hypothesize** how insect bodies changed over time.

THE FOSSIL RECORD

Scientists use the term "geologic time" to talk about Earth's history from its beginning to now. Each geologic time period has a name. The earliest insect fossils come from the Devonian period, which was from about 415 to 360 million years ago.

Scientists often use drawings like this one to show what ancient insects looked like.

▼

COMPRESSIONS AND REPLICATIONS

There are many kinds of insect fossils. Compressions form when an insect is pressed in **sediment** that becomes rock. These fossils may include just the exoskeleton or the insect's whole body.

Replications are copies of insect bodies or body parts made of minerals, or nonliving matter. They form as an insect's body breaks down over time. Minerals fill the space left by living matter. Insects that lived in the sea are often fossilized this way.

This fossil is a replication of a trilobite.

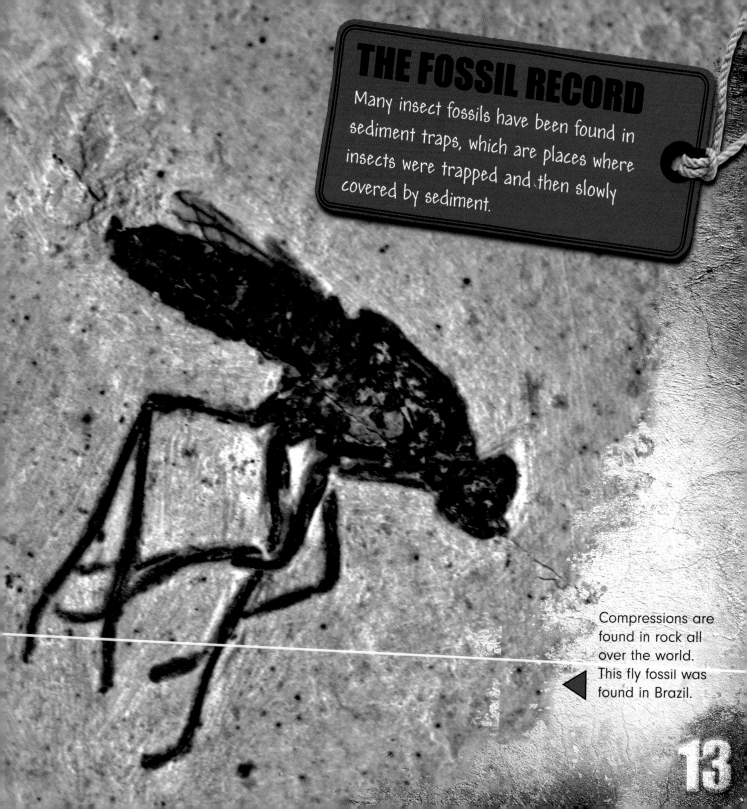

Many insect fossils have been found in sediment traps, which are places where insects were trapped and then slowly covered by sediment.

Compressions are found in rock all over the world. This fly fossil was found in Brazil.

AMBER AND IMPRESSIONS

Amber is resin, or a sticky matter that comes from trees, An amber inclusion is an insect that's trapped in ancient tree resin. The insect body is well preserved. Scientists have found amber inclusions that date back almost 300 million years.

An impression is a fossil made from a **mold**. The mold is created by the print of an insect's wing or other body part in mud. Over time, the mud with the impression turned to stone.

Some people wear amber inclusions as jewelry.

▼

Scientists study **trace fossils** to learn about how insects lived. These can be fossilized leaves that insects fed on or even little holes they dug.

FOSSILIZED WINGS

Impressions of wings are common insect fossils. Scientists use them to track the **development** of modern insect bodies. Fossils of insect wings date back about 350 million years. However, scientists think insects grew wings earlier. The earliest insects didn't have wings, but many of the fossilized wings scientists have found were well developed. No one knows what happened in between! Still, wing fossils are often complete enough to show what kind of insect they belonged to.

◀ Insect wings may be fossilized as compressions or replications.

THE FOSSIL RECORD

One of the oldest winged insects probably didn't use its wings for flying. Instead, it used them for gliding, or coasting, through the air.

Wing fossils are found most often because an insect's wings break down less easily than its other body parts.

LEARNING FROM FOSSILS

A fossil can tell scientists a lot about the insect it came from. Scientists use special methods to learn when the insect lived. They compare the insect's body parts to other fossils and modern insects. In this way, scientists figure out how ancient insects are linked to today's insects.

An insect fossil gives clues about an insect's individual features and actions, too. For example, if an insect fossil only has one set of footprints and no walking tracks, the insect that left the print probably could fly.

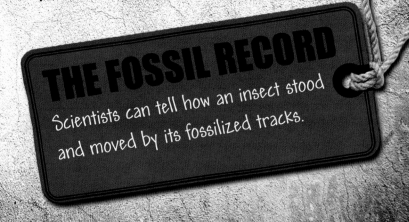

THE FOSSIL RECORD

Scientists can tell how an insect stood and moved by its fossilized tracks.

Insect fossils may be studied for many years before scientists are sure of the insect's place in history.

STILL EVOLVING

Insect fossils continue to change the way scientists view evolution. In 2004, scientists concluded that a set of insect jaws was 400 million years old. This means that insects appeared on Earth 10 to 20 million years earlier than scientists originally thought! In 2008, scientists found the oldest full-body impression of a flying insect yet. It is 300 million years old.

These finds are just the beginning. Scientists have so much more to learn from insect fossils.

These mosquitoes are fossilized in amber.

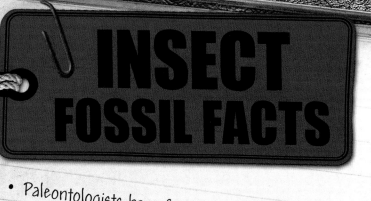

INSECT FOSSIL FACTS

- Paleontologists have found more than 100,000 preserved arthropods in the La Brea tar pits—a sediment trap in Los Angeles, California.

- Scientists have found insect inclusions in amber that are just a few hundred years old as well as inclusions that are millions of years old.

- One reason insect wings are common insect fossils is because animals that ate insects millions of years ago wouldn't eat the wings. Either their bodies couldn't break down the wings or they just didn't like the taste!

- Scientists believe that fossils show a linked evolution between insects and plants. As flowers grew, insects developed mouthparts to feed on them.

GLOSSARY

development: the act of growing and changing

evolution: the process of changes in a living thing that take place over many lifetimes

exoskeleton: an animal's hard outer covering

hypothesize: to make a guess based on facts

mold: a hollow form

preserve: to keep safe

sediment: matter, like stones and sand, that is carried onto land or into the water by wind, water, or land movement

species: a group of animals that are all of the same kind

trace fossil: a fossil that shows how an animal acted, such as footprints or tooth marks

FOR MORE INFORMATION

Books

Mitchell, Susan K. *Animals with Awesome Armor: Shells, Scales, and Exoskeletons.* Berkeley Heights, NJ: Enslow Publishers, 2009.

Spilsbury, Richard, and Louise Spilsbury. *Fossils.* Chicago, IL: Heinemann Library, 2011.

Websites

Let's Talk About Insects
urbanext.illinois.edu/insects/01.html
Find out more about insects in this fun slideshow.

Natural History Museum: Palaeontologist
www.nhm.ac.uk/kids-only/ologist/palaeontologist/
Learn more about the life of a paleontologist.

INDEX